SETTLEMENT
AND
SACRIFICE

Settlement
and
Sacrifice

The Later Prehistoric People of Scotland

Richard Hingley

Series editor: Gordon Barclay

CANONGATE BOOKS
with
HISTORIC SCOTLAND

THE MAKING
OF SCOTLAND

Series editor:
Gordon Barclay

Other titles available:

WILD HARVESTERS
The First People in Scotland

FARMERS, TEMPLES AND TOMBS
Scotland in the Neolithic
and Early Bronze Age

A GATHERING OF EAGLES
Scenes from Roman Scotland

First published in Great Britain in 1998
by Canongate Books Ltd, 14 High Street
Edinburgh E11 1TB

British Library Cataloguing-in-Publication Data
A catalogue record for this book is available on request
from the British Library

ISBN 0 86241 782 1

Series Design:
James Hutcheson, Canongate Books

Design:
Janet Watson

Printed and bound by
GraphyCems

Previous page
The 2000-year-old broch at Dun Dornadilla, Sutherland.
RCAHMS

Contents

Staircase
Mousa Broch,
Shetland.
HISTORIC SCOTLAND

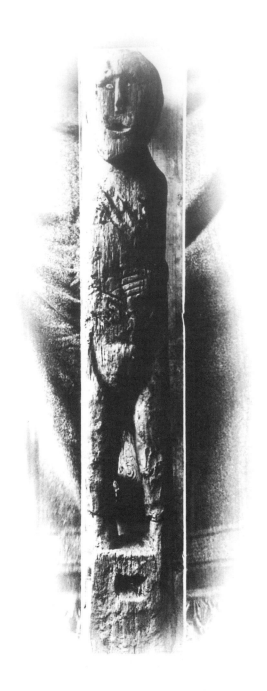

Ballachulish Figurine
A near life-sized wooden figure dating from around 600 BC.
NATIONAL MUSEUMS OF SCOTLAND

The Human Landscape

This book describes the people who lived in Scotland during later prehistory, the 1700 years between around 1500 BC and AD 200. The history of human settlement before this is covered by the titles *Wild Harvesters* and *Farmers, Temples and Tombs*, while *A Gathering of Eagles* gives an account of the Romans who invaded Scotland.

The landscape

The outline of Scotland and its islands would have been very similar to today, but in some places the sea has now moved further out from the shore (for instance, most of the mainland), while elsewhere it has cut into the land and ground has been lost (as in Orkney and Caithness).

However, the appearance of the land would have been very different then. At the beginning of the later prehistoric period parts of Scotland had been occupied for 3000 years or more by farmers who had cleared large areas of trees and made fields in which they planted crops and kept animals.

Some areas had not been cleared, and in others people had moved on and the trees had grown again, a process we call 'regeneration'. Other areas were covered in thick peat and the wet climate in later prehistory resulted in this bog spreading to areas that were previously lived in. Great difficulties were met with in travelling through mountains, bogs and woodlands which were inhabited by wild animals. These included bears and wolves which posed a threat to livestock and people, particularly children. The countryside was not, however, an untamed wilderness. The later prehistoric people had cleared large areas of land by this time, and we shall see that they lived a settled life and for the most part probably felt secure.

Later prehistoric people

It is often suggested that people at this time were warlike and fierce, but this is only part of the story; archaeological work tells us that they were also settled farmers who are likely to have welcomed gifts and tales from visitors from far afield. Until the invasion of the Romans, warfare was probably an occasional and small-scale activity.

The people of Scotland in later prehistory lived in well-built houses, usually circular, and the remains can be found over much of the country. In some places there were villages of roundhouses sometimes enclosed with a boundary. The people grew cereal crops in small fields; they also kept a range of livestock, including cattle, sheep, goats and pigs, and would have lived well on a diet of their own produce – meat, vegetables, bread and cheese supplemented by game, animals and fish.

Bronze Shield
A bronze shield from Yetholm, Roxburghshire which dates to around 800–700 BC. It is very well made but fairly fragile and was probably used for display rather than war.
NATIONAL MUSEUMS OF SCOTLAND

Later prehistoric people wore well-made clothes. They also had ornaments and weapons which displayed their wealth and status. Most of them probably lived their whole lives and died in the same area, but others would have travelled by foot, cart, horse and boat to visit neighbours and kin, or to trade. Life for these farmers was hard and usually fairly short by our standards. Many women and children died in childbirth and most people did not live beyond the age of 40. In these ways their way of life would not have been unfamiliar to recent generations of farmers in Scotland.

Although superficially similar to our recent ancestors in the basic ways of living and farming, some of their customs were very different, even strange, from our point of view. During the later part of our period, for instance, it is possible that when a member of the community died, the body was sometimes exposed on a wooden platform. When the dead body had decayed, the individual bones may have been removed and used in religious acts relating to the memory of the dead person. Occasional evidence suggests that people were even sacrificed to the gods.

They were creative and imaginative, not the primitives who are often portrayed in fiction and on television. Not only did they build complex and substantial houses, but they also made and owned some beautiful objects. Often these objects were deposited as offerings – sacrifices – to the gods. This book explains in more detail what these people were like, how they lived and how you can see and find out more about them.

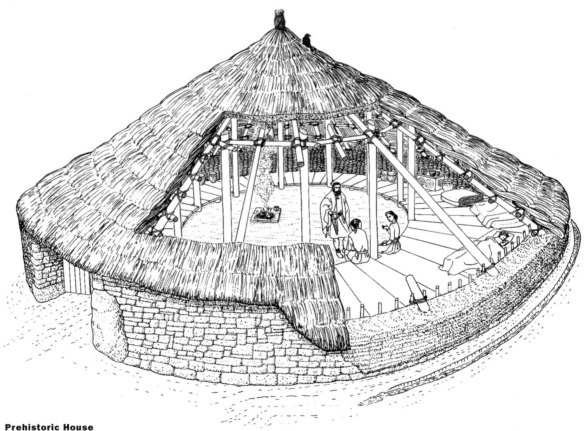

Prehistoric House

A house dating to about 3500 years ago at Lairg, Sutherland would have looked much like this. Many later prehistoric houses were circular, and were often very impressive and substantial.
CHRISTINA UNWIN: HISTORIC SCOTLAND

During the long period covered by this book there were many changes in the ways that people lived. At the start of later prehistoric times families still buried their dead relatives in substantial stone and earth burial monuments, but later, between 600 BC and AD 200, evidence for the ways in which the dead of the community were disposed of becomes less and less common.

By 1500 BC people were already building large roundhouses, but during the course of later prehistory many of these become more substantial and complex. At the beginning of our period people lived in unenclosed groups of round buildings, but from as early as 1000 BC they started to build various forms of enclosures around their settlements and some of these forts are quite substantial.

The objects that people used also changed through time. Weapons and other objects were common at the beginning and end of our period, but were not so common in between. The appearance of these objects changed according to fashion.

The physical geography meant that families in different parts of Scotland lived in quite different ways. A later prehistoric farm in Caithness would have looked very different from one on Lewis or in the Scottish Borders. Each part of Scotland had its own individual later prehistoric archaeological record.

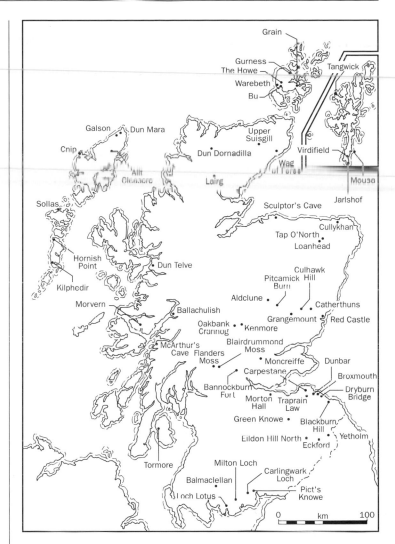

Distribution Map

This map shows the location of archaeological sites and finds which are mentioned in the book.

The People

Who were they?

Scotland as a political entity, where the people thought of themselves as Scots, did not exist until over 1000 years after the end of our period. The people who lived in the area of present-day Scotland during our period would have had a name, or series of names, for themselves and for their communities. We have no knowledge of what these were since nothing was written down and so there are no records which would tell us about the inhabitants. The names for groups of people, or 'tribes', were not recorded until Roman times.

This book will use the term 'later prehistoric' for the people I describe. When archaeologists talk about the period from around 1500 BC to AD 200 they often use the term 'Celtic'. The term

'Pictish' is also sometimes used in Scotland to refer to archaeological remains: for instance, brochs used to be known as 'Pictish towers'. Archaeologists also use the terms 'Iron Age' and 'Bronze Age'. What do these all mean?

The term 'Celtic' seems to me to be too ill-defined to be useful. It is applied to a whole range of people who lived across large areas of central and western Europe in later prehistoric times. In Ireland and western Scotland 'Celtic' is used to refer to a variety of monuments that date to a period of history later than that described in this book. The term is also used today by a range of people in western and north-western Europe, including Scotland, in order to identify themselves for cultural reasons.

Prehistoric People

Later prehistoric people from around AD 100. Two men on horse-back from north-eastern Scotland meet a woman and three men from the south of Scotland. People at this time dressed differently in various areas of Scotland to show their tribal identity. In addition wealthy and powerful people had access to more impressive ornaments, weapons and clothes. All of the people shown in this drawing are leading figures of the community, apart from a retainer who is looking after the horse. The artefacts shown mostly date from the last two centuries BC and the first two centuries AD. Those shown on the figures to the left have been found in north-eastern Scotland, with the exception of the pony cap, while those on the figures to the right have been found in southern Scotland.

CHRISTINA UNWIN

Later prehistoric people are also not likely to have thought of themselves as 'Pictish'. The Picts were a group of people who live across northern Scotland at a later date. They are first mentioned by a Roman author in the late third century AD, many years after the people discussed in this book were dead. The Picts were probably descendants of the later prehistoric people.

'Bronze Age' refers to the period in which people first used metal (around 2200-700 BC), the first metal in common use was bronze. The 'Iron Age' (around 700 BC-AD 400) was when iron was first used – a harder metal than bronze and considerably more difficult to work. These terms are used by archaeologists to relate to the adoption of certain technological skills, rather than to any real change in the inhabitants of Scotland during these periods. They would certainly have meant nothing to the later prehistoric men and women.

Who were these people? At one time it was thought that many waves of settlers had come to the British Isles, but there is no clear evidence for this, although individuals and groups will have travelled long distances on occasions. Most archaeologists now believe that the men and women who lived in Scotland at this time were descended from many generations who had lived in the same area. Although some new groups of settlers came to live in Scotland after AD 200, including the Scotti and the Vikings, many Scottish people today are likely to be descended from later prehistoric or even earlier inhabitants. If you are Scottish, you are probably descended at least in part from people who lived in Scotland at the time of the Roman invasion.

What did they look like?

We are dependent on the remains that these people left behind for an understanding of what they looked like. In very rare cases, peat bogs can preserve human bodies, including the skin, hair and internal organs. Preserved bodies have been found across Britain and northern Europe, including Scotland. They can tell us a great deal about diet and lifestyle during the later prehistoric period, but to date no Scottish examples have been studied using modern techniques.

Burials of people are more common, although still rare, as the majority of people do not appear to have been buried in a grave. It is usual for only the skeleton to survive as all the flesh has decayed and disappeared long ago. We know from skeletal evidence that later prehistoric people were probably not much smaller than we are. The analysis of 19 Iron Age burials which have been excavated on various sites throughout Scotland provides the following information. The 15 male burials suggest that adults males varied in height from around 1.65 metres

(5ft 5in) to 1.77 metres (5ft 9in). Female skeletons are rarer, but the four excavated examples vary from 1.52 metres (5ft) to 1.66 metres (5ft 5in) in height.

We can also say a little about the clothes and ornaments that these people wore. The Roman author Herodian wrote in the third century AD that people in northern Britain were for the most part naked. He also mentions that they tattooed their bodies with various designs and pictures of animals and that they possessed swords, spears, shields and iron ornaments. Herodian's is one of a number of accounts by Roman authors which dismiss the native people of Britain as uncivilised barbarians. The coldness of the climate suggests that most people dressed suitably for the elements.

Men, women and children wore woollen clothing to protect them from the cold and rain. They are also likely to have had linen, leather and skin garments. Clothing would have been carefully made and dyed in a variety of colours using natural dyes. They may have worn leather shoes, although none have been found so far. Men and women may have had different types of dress but we have very little information on this subject and so cannot be certain. In most situations, the wool and leather that the clothes were made from have disintegrated and leave no sign on an archaeological site. Where organic materials such as wool, leather and wood have fallen or been put into bogs or other wet areas, they are protected to a considerable extent from rotting by the limited supply of oxygen. The few discoveries of ancient clothes give us some idea what sort of clothes the people wore. For example, a hooded woven woollen garment found in Orkney was lost or deposited in a bog slightly

Skeleton

The skeleton of a man of about 35 to 45 years of age from the broch at The Howe, Mainland, Orkney. The dead body appears to have been left in a disused building prior to its collapse. Most of the bones of the body can be distinguished. The skull is to the right and has been crushed, while the remains of the leg bones are to the left.

HISTORIC SCOTLAND

Woollen Garment

A hooded woven woollen garment from Orkney, which was found in a peat bog. Radiocarbon dating suggests that this dates to just after the end of the time covered in this book, but people may have worn clothes of this sort during later prehistory.

NATIONAL MUSEUMS OF SCOTLAND

THE PEOPLE 13

Burnt Mound

Burnt mound at Tangwick, Eshaness, Shetland. A man is having a bath in the tank in the centre of the burnt mound. Burnt mounds may have been used for bathing or for cooking.

EASE

after the end of the later prehistoric period, but people will have worn clothes of this type earlier too. It is likely that the types of clothes worn at the beginning of later prehistory varied from those worn later. The clothes people are wearing in the illustrations of this book are based on the limited evidence from Britain and Europe.

The later prehistoric people are likely to have been careful of their appearances. Bronze mirrors of later prehistoric date have been found. Sharp bronze and iron tools were probably used during the later prehistoric period to cut hair and shave beards. Many men, however, may have grown beards and moustaches, and combs have been found that were probably used to groom them.

There is evidence that personal hygiene was important. Distinctive horseshoe-shaped piles of stones, called 'burnt mounds', date from 1200 BC to 700 BC. These mounds are formed from stones which have been heated or burnt and often contain evidence of a small tank of stone or wood. Similar arrangements used by North American Indians show that the stones were heated in a fire and placed in a water tank to create steam, forming a communal sauna where people washed and cleaned themselves. The heated water tanks may also have been used for cooking meat and vegetables. Burnt mounds are less common after about 700 BC, although large collections of burnt stones, which may represent bathing facilities, are sometimes found on settlement sites.

Mirror

A mirror from Balmaclellan, Kircudbrightshire which dates to the first century AD. These mirrors would have been used by important men and women.

NATIONAL MUSEUMS OF SCOTLAND

Personal ornaments were common during later prehistory, including a range of pins and bracelets, which are now over 3000 years old, used to fasten clothes and to keep hair in place. The massive armlets from north-western Scotland, torcs (neck rings), finger rings, pins, armlets, necklaces and brooches were worn 2000 years ago. Some of this metalwork was produced outside Scotland showing that contacts were made with friends, relations and traders in areas of southern Britain, Ireland and on the Continent. A bronze brooch from The Howe, a stone house in Orkney, was probably manufactured in southern Britain and brought into Scotland.

Some of the items of personal adornment were very valuable. The metal would have been expensive and some of the ornate objects must have required experienced specialists to produce them. Jewellery was also made in a range of other materials, such as bangles out of 'jet' and beads of glass. At the end of later prehistory, people wore different types of objects in various areas of Scotland, which suggests that people dressed in a way which showed which community they came from.

Armlet
Armlet in the form of a snake from Pitalpin, Angus. This item of personal adornment is probably about 1900 years old.
NATIONAL MUSEUMS OF SCOTLAND

How did they defend themselves?

From about 1500 BC to 600 BC a range of swords, axes, spears and shields made of bronze was used. An example is the bronze shield from Yetholm discussed earlier. Some of the weapons are (and always were) so fragile that they can only have been used for display, perhaps during ceremonies.

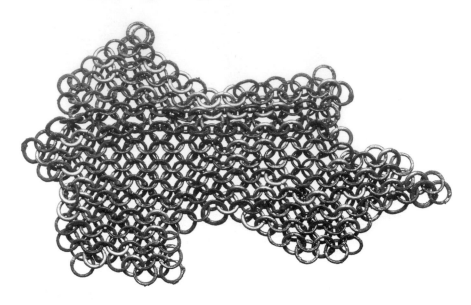

Chain Mail
A piece of chain mail from a collection of metal objects found in a peat bog at Carlingwark Loch.
NATIONAL MUSEUMS OF SCOTLAND

After this date, until the first century AD, people continued to make and use swords, spears and shields, particularly during the time of the Roman invasions. Some of these weapons would have been more effective in battle than earlier examples, since iron is far harder and longer-wearing than bronze. An example of chain mail was found in a peat bog at Carlingwark Loch, Stewartry, and this demonstrates that some later prehistoric warriors were quite heavily protected. Fittings for horse harnesses were also made by later prehistoric people and illustrate the widespread use of the horse both for riding and draught. Chariots drawn by horses may have been used in warfare.

It is usually assumed that men carried the weapons, but women may also have been armed. Whether people wore weapons whenever they were outside or only during battles and ceremonies is uncertain. Some of the more ornate weapons are likely to have been carried on special occasions by individuals to display their power and status in their local communities.

Scabbard
Sword scabbard from Morton Hall, Midlothian. This highly ornate object is made from bronze and is probably around 1900 years old. It is shown on the back of one of the men in the illustration on p11.
NATIONAL MUSEUMS OF SCOTLAND

What language did they speak?

These people may have spoken an early form of Gaelic, but whether any of the words used by modern Gaelic-speakers would have been understood by someone from the later prehistoric period is uncertain.

Were they healthy?

The bones from excavated human skeletons can yield a certain amount of information about the diseases and ailments from which these people suffered. The skeletons of a man and a woman found at Galson, Lewis, both showed signs of disease. The poorly developed enamel of the woman's teeth suggested that she had suffered childhood illnesses; slipped discs showed that she also suffered from back trouble. She had given birth to at least one child. The man had probably suffered back pain as he had two spinal conditions (Schmorl's nodes and spondylolysis) and also slight injuries to his spine.

A large stone cist found close to Dunbar in East Lothian contained the remains of at least 21 individuals, all of whom had unhealthy teeth. Tooth loss was not uncommon and chronic abscesses were fairly frequent. Dental decay, however, was not common, possibly due to the fact that people did not use sugar in their diet. Other common ailments included rheumatism, found in six of the East Lothian skeletons.

Not all later prehistoric people would have been unhealthy. Knowledgeable people were probably able to treat some health problems by the use of herbs, medicines and magic.

How long did they live?

Archaeology only provides a limited amount of evidence about how long these people lived. Although it is not possible to tell from their bones exactly how old someone was when they died, an estimate can be made. Analysis of the Dunbar burials provides the following information. The youngest male was 20 to 21 years old when he died, while the oldest was 35 to 40. The youngest woman was in her mid 20s at death and the oldest was about 40 to 50, which must have seemed a great age to these people. These young ages at death reflect the absence of modern standards of health care. Many mothers died in childbirth and death during infancy or early childhood would have been frequent. The remains of the young are rarely found, perhaps because there were particular ways for disposing of their bodies.

Pitcarmick Settlement

A later prehistoric settlement at Pitcarmick Burn, Perthshire. Several hut circles are visible to the bottom right of
the photograph and a series of cairns, linear dykes and other features can also be distinguished.
This is a very well preserved later prehistoric settlement which shows up well under a cover of snow.
RCAHMS

Farming and Eating

Most families had a staple diet derived from the meat of domestic animals and the crops that they had grown, supplemented by gathering wild fruits and plants, fishing and occasional hunting.

Patterns of farming

It is likely that almost all families at this time were involved in farming. People worked on the land, and probably had access to a particular area of arable and pasture land. We should not assume that families 'owned' land as we understand it, or that all cultivation plots were marked in a permanent way – in many societies where land is held communally, people are assigned different areas to cultivate every year. In such cases plots need not have been marked very clearly; at Upper Suisgill in Sutherland two plots were found separated only by a line of fist-sized stones.

In upland areas evidence of the fields that surrounded the settlements often survive. In rocky upland areas, people cleared the land of stones to create areas to grow crops. They placed the stones in small piles, which archaeologists call 'clearance cairns'. They also built field and yard walls using these stones. Elsewhere, especially in southern Scotland, people carefully ploughed along the contours of the hills to form level cultivation terraces. Across some parts of Scotland areas are covered in very narrow cultivation ridges which are formed of piled up earth. This is known as 'cord rig' and often appears to be of later prehistoric date. It has been suggested that cord rig was created by the use of spades and hoes, much in the same way that crofting cultivation was carried on into the twentieth century in the west and north of Scotland.

In these fields families planted, tended and harvested crops, which were then processed, stored and consumed. Barley was the main crop and wheat and oats were also grown. People used wooden ards (a simple plough which cut into and turned the soil) to till the fields. When iron became widely available towards the end of the later prehistoric period the ard was sometimes fitted with a metal tip to slice

Ploughing
A man ploughing with a wooden ard.
CHRISTINA UNWIN

into the soil more efficiently. People may have been able to cultivate some of the heavier more fertile soils of Scotland with these improved ards. However, iron plough tips are not frequently found in Scotland and simple wooden ards may have continued in common use; examples have been found in several places, such at Virdifield in Shetland and at Milton Loch in Dumfriesshire. In some places spades were used as cultivation tools, possibly to cut up the turf before the ard was used.

Grain was harvested by hand, possibly on occasion with the aid of bronze sickles. When archaeologists excavate sites they sometimes find grain which has been charred during processing.

Charred Barley
Charred barley found at the broch at The Howe, Mainland, Orkney. This barley would have rotted if it had not been charred.
HISTORIC SCOTLAND

Saddle Quern
Saddle quern in use. This comprises a simple, flattish, stone on which grain was ground using a smaller stone.
NATIONAL MUSEUMS OF SCOTLAND

Archaeologists often also find quernstones, grinding stones which were used to turn grain into flour. During the earlier part of our period crude saddle querns were used; while in the later prehistoric period more carefully prepared rotary querns become common. Two circular stones were fitted closely together, so that the upper one could be turned; grain was dropped down a hole in the middle of the upper stone onto the grinding surface on the lower stone and the resulting flour flowed out between the two. Bread, bannocks, gruel and porridge would have been produced from this flour, while barley, other cereals and wild plants may also have been fermented to produce alcoholic drinks.

Animal husbandry

Each family probably kept several different kinds of animal, although it is likely that the types and proportions kept would have varied between regions. Animal bones that have been found on excavated sites show that cattle, sheep, goats, pigs, dogs and horses were present. All of these animal types may have been eaten, as butchery marks were found on their limbs. Horses were ridden and harnessed to carts, and dogs were used for hunting, but even these animals may also have been eaten occasionally. At The Howe in Orkney evidence has been found that cats were kept, possibly to kill mice and for their fur, but they may also have been treated as domestic pets.

Hunting and gathering

In the Western Isles, deer bones are unusually common. Some of the weapons described in the previous chapter could have been used to hunt animals. Nevertheless, the small numbers of wild animal bones from sites suggest that hunting was in fact rare across much of Scotland. On other sites, bones sometimes survive to show that people fished and caught birds. Fishing was particularly important among mainland coastal communities and in the Western and Northern Isles.

During the excavation of Oakbank Crannog on Loch Tay in Perthshire, hazelnuts, cherries, blackberries and raspberries were found. The gathering of wild foods would have supplemented the diet of people throughout Scotland, particularly when the harvest was poor.

Deer
A 2000 year-old drawing of deer scratched on a piece of pottery from the wheelhouse at Kilpheder, South Uist. It is likely that deer were hunted in the Western Isles and formed an important part of the diet. This piece of pottery is reproduced near to its original size.
PREHISTORIC SOCIETY

Storing and cooking food

Later prehistoric people would have had a range of vessels for storing and for cooking food. In the Western and Northern Isles pottery vessels were in common use, as shown by small broken pieces of ceramics found during the excavation of houses. On occasions a whole vessel is found. Fewer pots were in use in mainland Scotland. People also used wooden and bronze vessels to store and process food. Evidence of wooden containers has been found in the remains of crannogs – houses built in lochs and bogs. Wood found deposited in waterlogged conditions can be remarkably well preserved.

In many later prehistoric houses the fire was lit on a single hearth set in the centre of the house, although occasionally a

house had more than one hearth. It is likely that each family cooked and ate food together, probably around the central hearth. Sometimes meat was cooked by placing it into a pit with hot stones or burning turf. Large groups of people met to eat communal meals on special occasions (this is described in more detail in on pages 46–8).

The end product

The evidence for farming, animal husbandry, hunting and gathering demonstrates the kinds of food which families ate. Another source of information for the diet of later prehistoric people is human excrement, or 'coprolites'. These have been found on a few sites, particularly those which have been damp and free from the oxygen which would lead to the decay of organic matter. The coprolites from Warebeth broch, Orkney, came from a number of individuals, probably including a child; one was deposited by an animal, probably a cat or a dog. All of the coprolites contained small quantities of plant remains, but the meals represented consisted mainly of meat; indicated by the presence of animal hairs and small pieces of bone. The animals eaten included red deer, sheep or goat, and birds; seeds within the coprolites included barley and linseed; while traces of peat probably indicated that food came into contact with the fuel of the fire during cooking. The animal dropping contained the eggs of a parasitic worm, but the human coprolites showed no evidence of parasites.

Coprolite Found at Warebeth
A piece of human excrement from Warebeth broch, Mainland, Orkney. Several coprolites were deposited in a well in the broch, presumably after it had ceased to be used, as it is not likely that the occupants would have fouled a source of water that was in use.
HISTORIC SCOTLAND

Making Things

All of the clothes and personal possessions described in the previous chapter, including the ards and quernstones used in the farming and processing of crops, and the pots and wooden vessels used in the storage and cooking of food, were made by later prehistoric people. Everyone within the community may have been involved in making objects. They used a range of locally available materials to make their possessions, but in some cases materials had to be brought into the community for the manufacture of particular items. Pots were produced from local clays and were hand-made and quernstones were usually cut from locally available coarse stone.

Iron and bronze

The production of iron or bronze objects may only have been carried out at certain times by specialists in metalworking. The ore required to produce bronze artefacts includes copper and tin; these are not common within Scotland and must have had to be brought into the communities when metal objects were required. Sufficient heat to melt the ore was created on a small fire. The ore was then melted in a clay container, or crucible, and poured into a mould to cool and produce a cast object. Remains of crucibles, moulds and slag (waste) from melting ores are found during archaeological excavations of later prehistoric settlement sites, demonstrating to the archaeologist that bronze objects were created by people at these locations.

Iron ore commonly occurs as bog iron across much of the country. This probably meant that there was no need to transport materials over such great distances as the constituents of bronze. The production of iron was a more difficult process than bronze-making and may have required specialist workers. The smelting of iron ore requires a very high temperature which could only be obtained by the construction of a clay-built furnace. Smelting involved melting the iron ore, producing a bloom, or cake of raw iron. The bloom was then worked into an artefact through a process called smithing. Both smelting and smithing are complex operations which require a good deal of knowledge. Smelting furnaces are found on occasions and slag, the waste product which results from both smelting and smithing, has been found on a range of later prehistoric sites. The iron artefacts which have been discovered include some very well-made items, indicating a high level of skill.

Pottery
A 3000-year-old pottery vessel from Allt Cleascre, Achmore, Lewis. The grain to the right of the pot was found inside it. The pot and grain were deposited in a peat bog as an offering to the gods or spirits.
NATIONAL MUSEUMS OF SCOTLAND

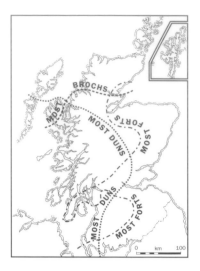

Settlement Map

Map of settlement zones in Scotland. People lived in different types of houses and settlements in different areas of Scotland and this map shows the main areas in which three types occur – brochs, duns and forts.

Houses

There is plentiful evidence from all over Scotland for the settlements and houses of later prehistoric people. If you live in or are visiting Scotland, it is likely that, wherever you are, you are within a kilometre or two of a farm or fort of this period. Different types of house and settlements occur in different areas. Many have been flattened by generations of ploughing and lie in fields, or are buried under modern towns and villages. Hundreds of these sites appear as 'cropmarks' in ploughed fields; the marks are revealed to archaeologists by aerial photography. Elsewhere in the lowlands archaeological evidence is often found during building work or where a quarry is being dug.

One of the remarkable features of Scotland's archaeology, in contrast to that of much of Europe, is that later prehistoric houses and settlements are very well preserved over large areas of the uplands because they were built of stone and have never been damaged or destroyed by later peoples' farms. Scotland has some of the most extensive and best preserved sites and structures of this date in western Europe. When they are excavated they can tell the archaeologist a great deal about our prehistoric ancestors.

Grangemount Cropmarks

Cropmarks of an open prehistoric settlement at Grangemount, Perthshire. The dark marks of ditches surrounding round houses and also souterrains are visible in the centre of the photograph (souterrains are described on p38).
RCAHMS

What types of houses did they live in?

The types of houses built and lived in by individual families varied from area to area, although most were circular in plan. This book focuses on the substantial roundhouses which were built across large areas of Scotland; these include roundhouses built of stone, timber (or both), crannogs, brochs, duns and wheelhouses.

Hut circle is the name for a class of monument which occurs across much of Scotland. They are one of the most common prehistoric archaeological remains in Scotland, found over much of upland Scotland at altitudes of up to 400 metres or more. They are common in Shetland, Orkney, the Western Isles, Caithness, Sutherland, much of the northern and western mainland of Scotland and the uplands of Perthshire. There are different types of hut circles in different parts of Scotland, and these were probably built throughout the later prehistoric period. The use of the term 'hut' is rather inaccurate, since many of these houses were large and complex. Although 'hut circle' is well established in the archaeological literature, it would be more accurate to use the term 'house circle'.

Broxmouth Settlement
The excavation of a later prehistoric settlement at Broxmouth (East Lothian). The site has been partly uncovered and traces of several circuits of enclosing ditches and also the slight foundations trenches of timber fences and small timber-built roundhouses are visible under excavation. The site was excavated in advance of quarrying.
RCAHMS

House Circle

A house circle under excavation at Tormore on Arran. The stone footings of a small circular house are visible.

HISTORIC SCOTLAND

(opposite)
Dun Dornadilla Broch

The broch at Dun Dornadilla, Sutherland. The entrance to the broch survives within part of the massive wall. Large parts of the broch wall have collapsed since it was built 2000 years ago but the scale of the surviving masonry is very impressive.

RCAHMS

The house circle was built in an area where stone suitable for building was plentiful and could be used for the walls. The remains of the house circles survive as low walls. On top of these stone foundations would have sat a wall built of turf or earth. The roof would have been constructed of timber covered with a thatch of heather or straw.

Early house circles in Scotland date to around 3800 years ago. Some large examples up to 15 metres across have been excavated, such as at Lairg in Sutherland (described on p.8), which were probably the homes of extended family groups. House circles often have a single central hearth which would have provided a source of heat and cooked food for the family.

Brochs were built mainly in the north and west of Scotland, but a few are known in eastern and southern Scotland. Generally they seem to have been built during the last two centuries BC and the first century AD, although some may be earlier. They are certainly the most impressive of the stone roundhouses which were built by the later prehistoric occupants of Scotland. The tallest surviving broch, Mousa, is over 13 metres high, and stands on a small island just off the mainland of Shetland. Many archaeologists, however, believe that the considerable height of

Mousa was not typical of all brochs. The walls of many other less well-preserved brochs were probably much lower, although they were still very substantial buildings.

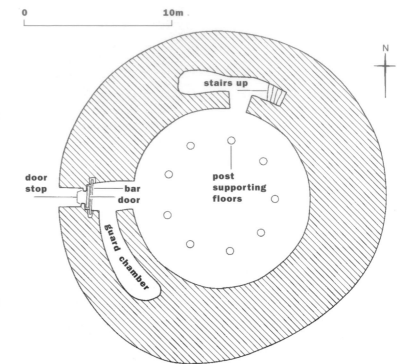

(right)

Dun Telve Floor Plan

Dun Telve, Glenelg, Lochalsh, Highland: the ground floor plan of the broch. Opening off the entrance, within the thickness of the wall, was a small chamber, often called the 'guard chamber'. From this small room a watch could be maintained over people entering, or attempting to enter, the building. There would have been a wooden doorway in the passage: traces of the way the door was fitted survive in most brochs.

CHRISTINA UNWIN

(below)

Broch at The Howe

Internal divisions inside the broch at The Howe, Mainland, Orkney. The circular area inside the wall of the broch was divided up by a number of stone partitions which formed private areas for members of the family. Some of the internal stone-built furniture is also visible.

HISTORIC SCOTLAND

Some brochs were built and lived in for a long period of time. At The Howe in Orkney roundhouses were built one on top of the other over a period of 500 years or more (between the eighth and fourth century BC and the first and second century AD), indicating a remarkable continuity of settlement.

Most brochs had at least two storeys, with a single low entrance on the ground floor through a passageway which passed through the thick wall. It is often necessary to stoop through this entrance to gain access into the interior. On emerging from the passageway and standing up straight a visitor would have entered into a dark space on the ground floor of the tall building.

The floor of the upper levels was built from timber and supported on a stone step

Staircase
Mousa Broch, Shetland. An exceptionally well-preserved 2000-year-old staircase in a broch wall.
HISTORIC SCOTLAND

called a 'scarcement' which is often visible in the surviving masonry of the broch as a continuous projecting ledge. This floor was also usually supported by a circle of internal posts. These wooden posts and the other wooden elements of the broch never survive, having decayed and collapsed soon after the abandonment of the structure. The broch at Dun Telve in Lochalsh, Highland, has two scarcements, suggesting that it had at least three floors including the ground floor. The first and second floors would have been accessible by a flight of stone steps built within the thickness of the broch wall; stone stairs survive in good condition on many broch sites. Brochs are thought to have had conical wooden roofs, probably thatched with straw from the fields, with heather from the moorlands, or with turf.

In Orkney and Caithness stone partitions and furniture often survive on the ground floor, showing that in these cases the main living area may well have been on this level. There would be private areas where people could eat, sleep and undertake other activities. Often a hearth was placed in the centre of the floor.

Dun Telve

Dun Telve: a view showing how the broch would have looked after it was built. It was a massive stone building which would have impressed both visitors and occupants.
CHRISTINA UNWIN

What Were Brochs For?

In the past it was thought that brochs were built solely to protect the occupants. They were imposing stone structures with no windows and only a single entrance. However, they do not make very much sense in terms of formal warfare, because they could not withstand any form of prolonged siege. Although some brochs have wells, many are without a source of fresh water. Even if fresh water was available within the broch, attackers could have driven off some of the livestock remaining outside, since it is unlikely that all the cattle of a family or community could have

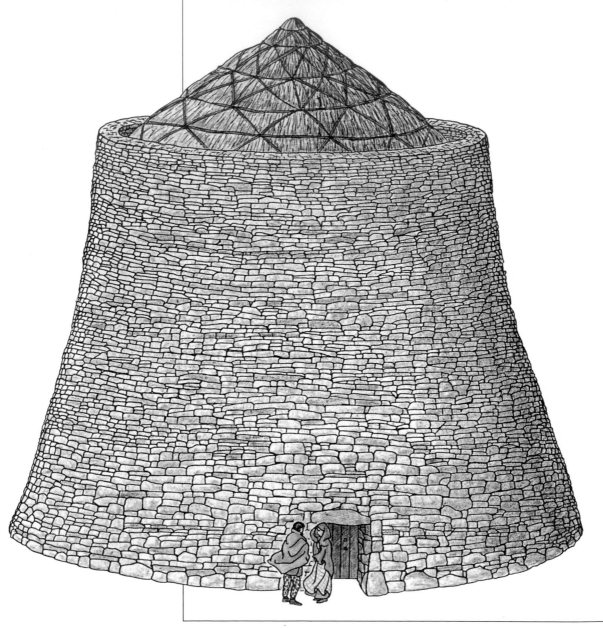

been brought inside the broch for protection. Attackers could have burnt the crop belonging to the broch family, who would then have been likely to die of starvation in the winter. In a similar way to the late medieval Scottish towerhouses, brochs

were probably intended to impress others, although they would also have served to protect their occupants from small-scale raids. They are often built on low hills, which would have served to have made them even more impressive.

Dun Telve Cross-section

Dun Telve: a cross-section showing the broch in use. The ground floor space was probably a byre for the cattle of the family and the living space would have been on the first floor level of the broch. This living area probably had a central hearth and wooden partitions dividing up the living and sleeping area. The second floor might have been used for storage.
CHRISTINA UNWIN

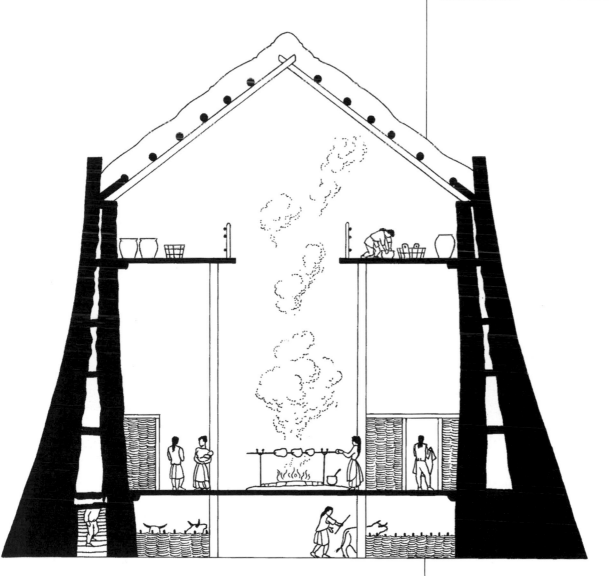

Dun houses. In Argyll, Galloway and across parts of Central Scotland, the remains of substantial circular stone-built houses are often called 'duns'. Many of these are large house circles which are not quite as complex as the brochs. They are often placed on the top of hills, helping to make them more imposing. When excavated, as in the case of the two houses at Aldclune, Perthshire, duns turn out to have been substantial and complex roundhouses built of stone and timber, with wooden roofs covered in thatch. They often do not contain the staircases that occur in brochs and many may only have been of one storey.

Wheelhouses. The wheelhouse is another distinctive type of later prehistoric roundhouse. They are called 'wheelhouses' because they look like a spoked wheel in plan. Within the area defined by the stone walls there were stone pillars which supported the roof. These stone pillars resemble the posts in some timber houses (*see below*). Wheelhouses were built during the last few centuries BC and first century AD in the Western Isles and Shetland and perhaps in other areas of Scotland. Some of them are particularly well preserved because they were built by digging into sand-dunes, and often filled with sand after they were abandoned.

Timber roundhouses. Elsewhere in southern and eastern Scotland, where stone was less available, later prehistoric roundhouses were often built in a different way. The walls of these houses were of timber, daub and earth and they are inevitably less well preserved, although careful excavation can tell us about the people who built and inhabited them. Unlike the upland house circles, there is usually very little or no trace of the later prehistoric timber roundhouse in the landscape today.

Some of the timber houses may have been built to last, although there is considerable

Wheelhouse
The wheelhouse at Jarlshof, Shetland. The stone pillars that held up the roof are visible and you can see out through the door of the house. The roof was probably covered with timber and thatch, but this has long since decayed.
HISTORIC SCOTLAND

controversy about how long such houses would have stood –
some archaeologists propose no more than 50 years, while others
compare them with medieval timber buildings and suggest a far
longer period.

Many of the examples which have been excavated do not fall
into easily identifiable types. Excavation in many cases uncovers
evidence for a ring of post-holes which would have held the
bases of upright timbers that supported the walls of the house.
Other houses had walls constructed of timbers which were
placed in slots cut into the ground in the form of a circle. The
long timbers which could be cut from the woodland in these
areas meant that houses of great diameter could be built; some
are more than 20 metres in diameter, although there are many
houses of smaller size. Both types of house often have an internal
ring of post-holes which contained timbers supporting the roof
and possibly an upper floor.

One particular type of roundhouse which has been defined
and studied in some detail is the 'ring-ditch house', examples of
which have been excavated in
East Lothian and Angus. The
interior of the house closest to
the wall was dug into the
ground and often paved, while
the central part of the house
comprised a raised area. It has
been suggested that the paved
floor of the ring-ditch house
was a byre for cattle and that
the family occupied the first
floor level. Ring-ditch houses
were commonly built around
500 BC.

Many other timber houses
probably had second floors,
although the traces of central
fireplaces in some of them
indicate that the ground floor
was not always a byre, and that
the family's accommodation
may have been divided
between two floors. On
occasions the roundhouse
was located in an prominent
position in the landscape, as
in the case of the recently
excavated ring-ditch house at

Wheelhouse Plan
A wheelhouse at Kilphedir, South Uist.
The plan and a cross-section drawing of
this well-preserved building shows how it
was built and also why buildings of this
type are know as 'wheelhouses'.
PREHISTORIC SOCIETY

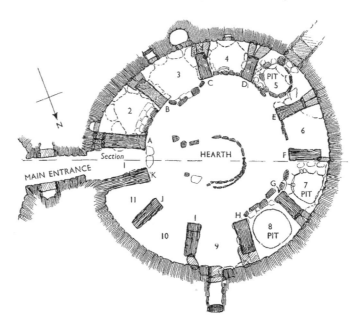
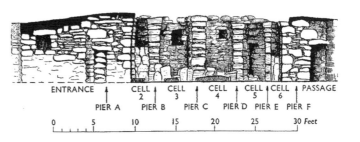

Culhawk Hill in Angus. This large house would have dominated the landscape and the valley below.

Bannockburn House

A later prehistoric house at Bannockburn Fort, Stirling, under excavation. The house was defined by a timber slot which held the wooden outer wall. There were also several circles of vertical posts set in post-holes within the house which held up the roof and possibly a timber first floor. The relative size of the people excavating the house shows how large it would have been.

HISTORIC SCOTLAND

Crannogs. Across Scotland, particularly in the Highlands and south-west, timber roundhouses called 'crannogs' were built on artificial platforms of wood and stone constructed in lochs and bogs. The name 'crannog' is derived from the Gaelic term 'crann', which means 'wood'. Usually a wooden causeway links the crannog to the shore. Crannogs appear to have been built throughout later prehistoric times and were also occupied and built in medieval Scotland.

The reasons that led people to build houses in the middle of lochs are unclear. Living in a crannog in the winter must have been difficult, with cold air blowing off the loch. In the same way that roundhouses and brochs were often located on the tops of hills in order to command the surrounding landscape, the location of the crannog would have created a major impression on visitors, and have made the occupants feel secure.

Owing to the effects of waterlogging the wooden objects used by the occupants and the rubbish accumulated during the occupation of the house are often very well preserved and tell us a great deal about the lives of people at this time. The evidence from Oakbank Crannog, Perthshire, for the diet of its occupants

Crannog
Reconstruction drawing of the crannog at Milton Loch, Dumfries, under construction. This crannog was a large wooden house built upon a stone and timber island in the loch. The ~~models are based loosely on the example found at Loch Lotus in Dumfries~~

CHRISTINA UNWIN

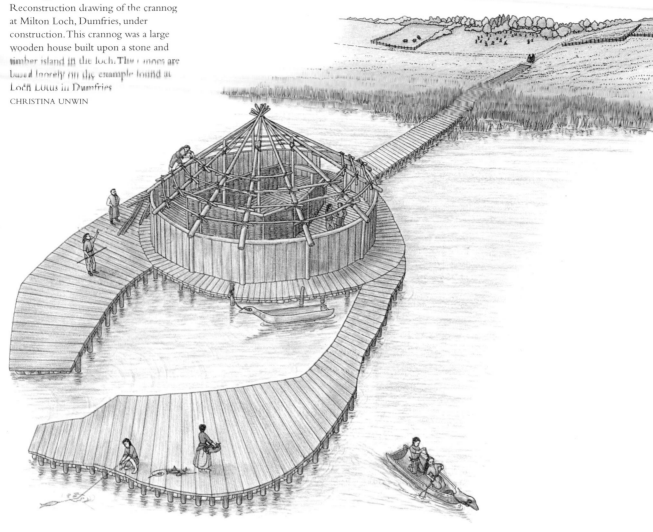

has already been described in on page 21. A crannog has been reconstructed in Loch Tay, close to Kenmore, Perthshire and can be visited by the public.

How many people lived in a house?

The basic structure of most stone and timber roundhouses was very similar, with a wall supporting a roof and often with an internal ring of timber posts or stone columns providing extra support. Some of these houses had upper floors. They varied considerably in size: some are as small as 4 metres in diameter, but many are very substantial, up to 22 metres across.

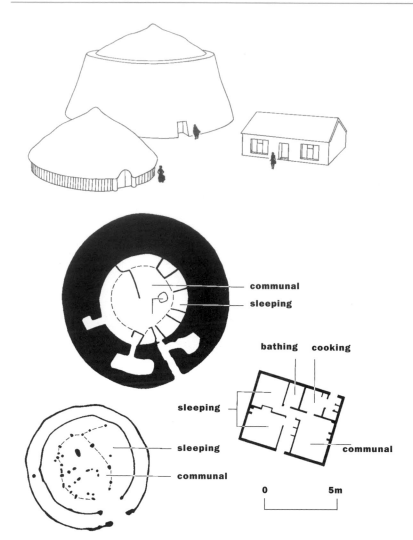

There is enough space in the average broch, or roundhouse, for quite a large number of people to live, especially if the building had an upper floor. The size of the family group in one of the larger timber roundhouses of southern Scotland may have been at least as large as that of the broch-dwelling family, due to the fact that the internal space within a timber house is often greater than the more northerly stone buildings. Some houses might have contained large and complex family groups of perhaps as many as 30 people, or more. As we have seen, in some cases cattle may have shared the family accommodation, a tradition which continued in some areas of Scotland until the beginning of the twentieth century.

House Comparison

A comparison of later prehistoric houses with a modern house shows how substantial these houses were. The large stone house is based on Bu, Orkney, the timber house on a house from Dryburn Bridge, East Lothian and the modern house was built just after the Second World War.

CHRISTINA UNWIN

The family and their home

By studying modern farming societies, we can see that the interiors of these later prehistoric houses would have been organised in very complex ways. Certain areas were set aside for different members of the family, perhaps older members or different sexes. The stone and timber partitions in brochs, wheelhouses and other roundhouses may reflect this. The majority of the stone and timber roundhouses of Scotland have a single doorway, usually facing the direction of the rising sun, to the south or south-east. It has recently been suggested that the occupants did different things at different times thoughout the day in various parts of the house.

The families who lived in these houses were very different from families today. Various Roman literary sources tell us about family groups in northern Europe; they suggest that families were

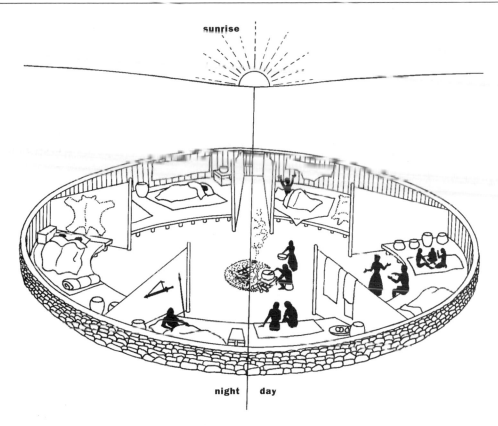

sunrise

night | day

Roundhouse
A diagram to show the internal organisation of a roundhouse. Eating and daytime activities may have occurred in the south of the house, storage and sleeping to the north.
CHRISTINA UNWIN

organised according to marriage rules which enabled every man to have more than one wife (polygamy), but it is also possible that a woman might have had several husbands (polyandry). The exact organisation of the family is unclear.

Several generations of a single family probably lived in a single house. Owing to the fact that life-expectancy was fairly short, adult responsibilities, marriage and childbearing started earlier than in our society; grandparents, where they survived, may often have lived with their children. If a couple had several offspring, it is fairly likely that their children and their own families would have lived together in one house, or in a group of houses. Many of these roundhouses also had a single central hearth, a communal focus where the family who lived in the house ate and sat. At Aldclune in Perthshire, one of the two houses had four hearths, each of which may have been used by a single family group, or by different parts of a single family.

Whether the property – the house, the fields and the animals – passed from fathers to sons, from mothers to daughters, or a mixture of both, or was even held communally is uncertain. Although it has usually been assumed that property passed from fathers to sons, this reflects more, perhaps, how our own society was organised until recently; there is no reliable evidence that this is what happened in the past.

What Are Souterrains and What Were They Used For?

Souterrains are stone-walled underground passageways which occur mainly in Angus, Aberdeenshire, Sutherland and Caithness, and in the Northern and Western Isles. They are usually attached to a stone or timber roundhouse. In the past all sorts of explanations were put forward to explain why souterrains were built; it was even suggested that they were refuges in time of trouble, although this is unlikely because once entered there was often no other way out. Since these underground chambers maintain a constant low temperature, even in very hot weather, it is likely that they were often used for storage, perhaps for meat and cheese. The souterrain at Newmill in Perthshire was connected with a timber house and had two entrances – one from the house, the other from the outside. The excavator suggested that it was used to store grain – at harvest time the grain was put into the souterrain through the outside door and then brought into the house as needed through the connecting door. The idea that some souterrains were used to store grain is supported by the excavated evidence from Red Castle in Angus, where charred grain was found on the souterrain floor. Some of the Angus souterrains are so large that they may have been used as central stores for a community.

It is possible that souterrains have a religious significance, but their exact meaning to later prehistoric people is uncertain. However, the use of a souterrain as a store does not preclude the idea that it might also have been a shrine. The storage of crops though the winter must have been vital for these later prehistoric people and the souterrain therefore would have been associated with magical powers because it was a container and preserver of an essential resource.

Souterrain
The souterrain at Grain, Mainland, Orkney. This is a carefully built stone cellar with pillars that held up the roof. The metal bar has been put into the souterrain in recent years to help to hold the roof up.
HISTORIC SCOTLAND

Settlements

Different types of settlements were built in Scotland during later prehistory. At the start of our period it would appear that most of the population lived in open settlements of clusters of roundhouses, but around 1000 BC people began to build enclosure walls, palisades, or banks and ditches around their settlements.

The open settlement

This was usually made up of a group of houses of similar size, with no obvious indication that any one family was dominant. They varied in size from a single isolated house to loosely associated groups of up to 20 houses and sometimes quite large villages were formed. The individual houses lay within their fields with no prominent enclosure boundary, although in some cases houses were separated from their fields by walls. Some survive as earthworks, while others have been ploughed-out and are only shown by cropmarks. The settlements at Green Knowe in Peebleshire and Lairg in Sutherland are Bronze Age open settlements. During the Iron Age, people in some areas, for instance in Fife and parts of Perthshire, continued to live in these unenclosed settlements.

Green Knowe Settlement

The open settlement at Green Knowe, Peebleshire. This was occupied for some time around 3000 years ago. A number of small roundhouses are spread along the hillside, each one built on a small platform. The fields and pasture areas used by each family occur around the houses and are defined by stone dykes.

CHRISTINA UNWIN

The enclosed settlement

Around 1000 BC a new type of settlement – the enclosed settlement – began to appear. They occur across most of Scotland, although only occasionally in the north, and are very common in some areas such as the Borders, East Lothian and Argyll. They vary in scale from small farms to large hillforts. We have seen that some open settlements were divided from their fields by walls, but in the case of enclosed settlements a single bank, ditch, wall or palisade surrounded the whole of the site. This type of enclosure can be compared with a hedge or with a stone or brick wall around a modern house and garden, although some of these enclosures were very substantial and defined the outer edge of the settlement in an imposing way. There was a great variety of enclosed settlements but few have been excavated. The available evidence suggests that enclosed settlements were built from 1000 BC until the first century BC/first century AD, but there was a later revival after the Romans had left Scotland.

Enclosures consisting of a palisade of vertical timbers may have occurred at an early date on many sites. Walls around settlements are common where stone is easy to acquire, particularly in Argyll, the west coast of the Highlands and on the islands. These are often called 'duns'; as we have seen, many duns were large roundhouses while others were enclosed groups of houses. In southern and eastern Scotland people built stone walls where stone was available, but in other areas they built earth banks reinforced with timber. Many of the settlements with earth banks also had ditches outside the bank; the banks were formed by the material thrown up when the ditch was dug. Sometimes only cropmarks indicate the location of these sites.

Most enclosed settlements had a single entrance, in some cases a simple break in the ditch, bank or wall; on the more impressive settlements a stone or timber gate was constructed. Traces of such gates are sometimes found when the sites are excavated, as at Cullykhan in Banffshire where a timber gate was built across the entrance passageway.

Dun Mara

A small enclosed settlement at Dun Mara, Lewis. The dun is visible on the coastal headland and it is enclosed by a stone wall. Traces of post-medieval cultivation are visible inland from the dun.

HISTORIC SCOTLAND

Enclosed settlements were built in different kinds of places. Many were built on the tops of hills, others on hill slopes, and occasionally they occur on low ground. Some enclosed sites are located on coastal promontories and these are often called 'promontory forts' or 'cliff castles'.

Enclosed settlements could contain a single house but many have between two and ten individual houses, each of which may have housed a single related family and which together made up a community. The family of an individual's brother or sister, or aunt or uncle, for example, may have lived in a separate house but within the same enclosure. At Gurness in Orkney the broch dominates a surrounding group of smaller houses within the same enclosure; here the leading family of the community possibly lived in the broch.

The largest of the enclosed settlements were the hillforts, which had strong defences protecting the settlement. The largest and most impressive examples include Eildon Hill North (Ettrick and Lauderdale), Traprain Law (East Lothian) and Tap O'Noth (Aberdeenshire). Eildon Hill North is over 16 hectares in extent and enclosed as many as 296 individual house platforms, each the location of a small roundhouse. Limited archaeological excavation suggests that the hillfort may have been constructed around 1000 BC and that the houses were not all in use at the same time. It may have been abandoned at some stage, after which it appears to have been re-occupied in the period of Roman occupation during the second and third centuries AD. Traprain Law is almost as extensive as Eildon Hill North and appears to have had a similarly early origin. Again there is a lack of clear evidence for occupation between around 600 BC and 50 AD, although we know that activity occurred on the hilltop during the Roman period because finds of this date have been made. The Brown and White Caterthuns in Angus are also impressive hillforts. Recent excavation on the Brown Caterthun indicates that the earliest rampart was built between 700 and 500 BC, although the hill was refortified on a couple of occasions during the time when Eildon Hill North and Traprain Law appear to have been unoccupied.

Cropmarks

Cropmarks of the enclosed settlement at Carperstane, East Lothian. This is a very regular, circular enclosed settlement with at least three circuits of enclosing ditches. The banks have been ploughed out and the ditches infilled. The parallel vertical lines at the top of the photograph are the results of modern drainage while those at the bottom are a result of the way in which the field is currently being cultivated.
RCAHMS

(above)
Gurness
Air photograph of the broch and
settlement at Gurness, Mainland, Orkney.
The large broch is surrounded by a
number of smaller buildings and a
series of enclosing banks and ditches.
RCAHMS

(opposite)
Eildon Hill Hillfort
The hillfort at Eildon Hill North, Ettrick
and Lauderdale. The ramparts of the fort
are visible running around the hill. In
the interior to the left are faint traces of
the platforms left by hundreds of small
houses.
HISTORIC SCOTLAND

Why did some families enclose their settlements?

It is not certain why families in some areas of Scotland built walls and banks around their settlements and others did not. It used to be thought that settlements were enclosed to defend their occupants against the advancing Romans, but we now know that many of the sites date back to at least 1000 years before the Roman invasion, while others are later but were either abandoned or their defences disused by the time of the Romans.

It has also been suggested that worsening environmental conditions around 1000 BC made farming in many upland areas impossible, so that more people needed farmland in lowland areas. Families therefore needed to define and defend their settlements and land from neighbours by building boundaries. Nevertheless, this only occurred in some areas. In some parts of Scotland the contrast is very clear – for instance, to the south of the Firth of Forth, in East Lothian and the Borders, enclosed settlements are very common, while to the north, in Fife, Angus and parts of Perthshire, almost all settlements are open. It is unclear why the population in East Lothian would have required defending while those in Fife were quite happy to live undefended. It is possible that people in later prehistory merely had a tradition of doing things differently in different areas – building enclosures may merely have been a matter of choice.

Perhaps the impressive roundhouses and enclosed settlements were built for the same basic reasons, individual status and group identity. Previously archaeologists have seen both types as solely defensive. It is just as likely, however, that both substantial roundhouses and enclosed settlements helped families to define the identity of the group to which they belonged. Substantial roundhouses and most of the enclosed settlements probably formed the homes for individual families, while some of the more extensive enclosed settlements and open settlements probably formed the homes or the meeting places for extensive communities.

Neighbours and Friends

Having considered some of the houses and settlements in which families lived, we also need to look at how they related to their neighbours. The population of Scotland as a whole was not as substantial as it is now, although large numbers of later prehistoric houses occur in some areas and many areas of the country were more heavily populated than they are now.

Travel

Many of the objects owned by families were transported over great distances – weapons and ornaments found in Scotland show similarities to objects elsewhere in Britain and further afield. This means that some people did travel around and would have carried news and ideas with them as well as objects.

Boggy areas, forests and mountains would have presented considerable obstacles to travellers and visitors in many parts of Scotland. There were no well-made roads and the tracks were unpaved. In some boggy areas wooden trackways were built to help people to cross marshes, such as those found during peat-cutting in Flanders Moss and Blair Drummond Moss, Stirlingshire. Such causeways were not common, however, and most transport would have taken place along dirt tracks which in the autumn and winter must have been very muddy.

Travel would have been easier by water than by land. Families who lived by lochs, rivers or the sea would have had boats for transport and fishing. Different types of boats, including dug-out canoes, have been found preserved in bogs in Scotland and finds from elsewhere in Britain show that more substantial seagoing boats travelled along major rivers, up the coast and across to the islands, Ireland and northern Europe.

Wooden Trackway
A prehistoric wooden trackway known as the Eclipse Track in Somerset, England. The Scottish prehistoric trackways found in Flanders and Blairdrummond Moss might have looked very similar when they were uncovered in the late eighteenth century.
SOMERSET LEVELS PROJECT

Were Large Hillforts Towns?

Some of the largest of the enclosed settlements are so extensive that there is a tendency to view them like modern towns. Eildon Hill North had a large number of roundhouses and the hillfort of Traprain Law had an area equivalent to the medieval centre of the neighbouring market town of Haddington. It has been suggested that some hillforts in the south of Britain served, in effect, as towns for their surrounding populations: that they were places in which people bought and sold goods and were also perhaps local centres of government and the homes of important chieftains.

There are several problems with this explanation. No large hillforts have been excavated on any scale in Scotland but, when similar sites have been excavated in the south, the materials they produce are very similar to those from other typical farms. Large hillforts do not necessarily appear to have been production centres for pots, ironwork or clothes. There is also very little evidence that they were places in which items were bought and sold, or that they were the homes of important individuals. The excavated evidence often suggests that they were just very extensive enclosed settlements and possibly meeting places.

Marriage and kin

The population of later prehistoric Scotland did not live in towns and cities. Some communities lived in groups of houses, others were dispersed in the countryside. Individual families would have had a network of kin and a range of friends in their neighbourhood and further afield, who would have helped to provide security if the harvest was bad and physical protection in times of unrest. Children eventually needed to find partners in order to raise their own offspring. Every society has taboos about who precisely can be married – we do not permit the marriage of brother and sister for example, but in some societies people are forbidden to marry even more distant relations such as first or second cousins, and so the availability of possible marriage partners who are unrelated becomes a matter of great significance.

Fairs and festivals

If they were not towns, what function did these large hillforts have? An alternative opinion is that they were places in which people gathered to celebrate festivals or to deal with disputes or legal matters. Goods might have been exchanged and alliances made between families at these times. The houses within the hillforts may have served as accommodation during the festivities. The large number of houses at Eildon Hill North may indicate that many families were involved, drawn from a wide area. Gatherings may have occurred throughout the year, but were probably more common and popular at times when the demands of agricultural life were not too great.

The houses at these hillforts would therefore have been for temporary occupation only, similar to the 'booths' or the temporary houses set up on the same site every year by the same families at the law gatherings of the Norse settlers over 1000 years later. It is also possible that families retreated to these places in times of war, which may be the reason why they are defended by ramparts.

Gatherings of populations may also have occurred in other places, including the houses and enclosures around settlements. Some of the brochs of the north and west of Scotland are so substantial that they were probably built by a number of families who would have co-operated over the gathering of stone, wood and other materials required to build the structure. The construction of the building was also a major operation and may have involved large groups. Some of the other roundhouses may also have been built by groups of families: for example some pits in the floor of the wheelhouse at Sollas on North Uist contained

Traprain Law Hillfort

The hillfort at Traprain Law, East Lothian. Two ramparts are visible on the right (north) of the hill. Modern quarrying has cut into the hill causing much damage.
RCAHMS

(inset)

Trapain Law Model

A reconstruction of Traprain Law 2000 years ago. Several circular houses have been built in the fort, a gathering of people is occurring close to the top of the hill, while a large fire is burning on the top point of the Law. Traprain Law may have been a place where people met to celebrate festivals. These festivals may have lasted for several days – food and alcoholic drinks would have been consumed.
CHRISTINA UNWIN

the remains of animals which may have been part of a meal partaken by those who gathered to build the house. The burials of a horse under the rampart of the hillfort at Eildon Hill North may represent the remains of a meal eaten by those who built the rampart. The animal remains may also have been in part an offering to the gods, with choice parts of the animal buried or burnt in dedication (see next chapter).

Families may therefore have met for a number of reasons: to celebrate, to build houses or settlements, and probably to exchange produce and stories. Other gatherings probably occurred at particular times, such as the birth and death of members of the community. They may also have occurred at significant spots when groups of people met to make offerings to the gods.

Tribes

We have seen that people lived dispersed throughout the countryside, but loose groupings of families probably felt kinship even in times of peace, an association reinforced by attending meetings. At times of crisis individual families may have gathered together into tribes in order to fight incomers, their leaders having access to impressive swords, shields and ornate personal ornaments, even in times of peace. These metalwork objects displayed the wealth and power of these leaders of the community. The evidence for the dominant broch and surrounding settlement at Gurness may also indicate the existence of a dominant individual and subservient families.

The Roman author Ptolemy wrote down the names of a number of 'tribes' who occupied northern Britain at the time of the Roman occupation. During the Roman invasion in AD 83 native people combined to fight the Roman forces at Mons Graupius under a leader called Calgacus. He led soldiers from a number of different tribes, and it took serious military aggression from the Romans to force the natives to co-operate in this way.

Ptolemy's Map

Map of the 'tribes' of Iron Age Scotland as recorded by the Roman author Ptolemy. These tribes may have been groups of families who felt that they were descended from a common ancestor. They may even have had tribal meetings at the major hillforts or elsewhere.

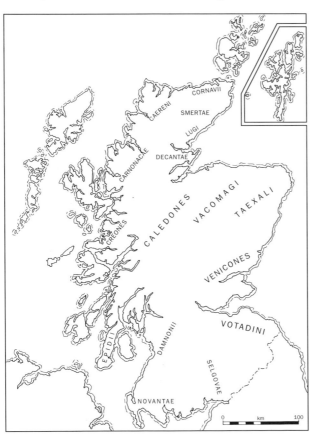

Sacrifice and Religion

It is difficult to say very much about how later prehistoric people thought and what they believed in. They had no writing and did not record their thoughts and beliefs, but it seems certain that they had a strong oral tradition. They passed on stories, medical knowledge, hunting lore and traditions from one generation to the next, as well as attending to the important matters of naming of places and detailing events which happened at them. Older men and women would have been revered as a source of knowledge and because of their long experience.

The gods

It is probable that they believed in gods, a range of spirits or divine beings who controlled the seasons and the productivity of crops and the animals upon which communities depended. In an age before anyone had a detailed understanding of nature, many aspects of the changing seasons and the growth of crops and animals must have appeared largely beyond the control of the community, and revering the gods would have provided one way of trying to ensure good harvests and a ready supply of food. A wooden figure, found during peat cutting in a bog at Ballachulish near Fort William (Lochaber) in the nineteenth century, may represent a figure of a god.

In earlier periods of Scotland's prehistory, religious activity was centred around burial sites, stone circles, henges and standing stones. In later prehistory these sites fell out of use, although many show signs of later activity, such as metalworking in the stone circle at Loanhead in Aberdeenshire and the henge at Moncreiffe in Perthshire. The Roman authors Caesar and Tacitus mention that druids existed in Britain and on the Continent. The druids appear to have been a group of religious specialists and it is possible that such figures may have existed among the communities of Scotland.

Offerings to the gods

Crops and animals were vital for survival and so it is thought that later prehistoric communities had a range of beliefs relating to the fertility of crops and stock. Significant items are often found in archaeological excavations, such as the remains of a horse buried beneath the rampart at Eildon Hill North, and animal and human bones under the floor of the wheehouse of Sollas on North Uist. Quernstones, used to grind corn, may have also been placed in certain places for religious reasons. At Aldclune in Perthshire numerous quernstones were incorporated into the

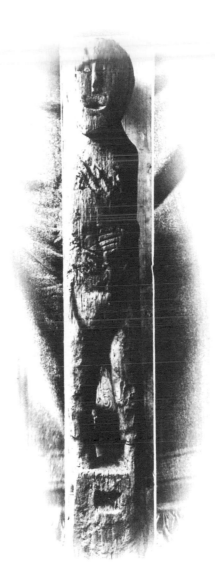

Wooden Figurine
The Ballachulish figurine which was found close to North Ballachulish, Lochaber. It is an almost life-sized wooden figure of a woman dating to around 600 BC who may have been a goddess or spirit.
NATIONAL MUSEUMS OF SCOTLAND

floors of two houses, while at Pict's Knowe in Dumfriesshire quernstones and other objects were found in the ditch of an enclosure which was dug in the first or second century AD and seems to have been built into the remains of a Neolithic henge. These items may have been deposited as offerings to the gods or spirits.

Later Roman writers tell us that the peoples of north-western Europe revered watery places and groves of trees as places of communication with their gods. It is likely that later prehistoric communities in Scotland gathered at places such as the peat bog at Ballachulish Moss to worship. We know this because of the range of items deliberately dropped or thrown into the Scottish wetlands. Some of these are domestic items, such as wooden containers, often packed with a substance called 'bog butter'. Wooden containers full of this substance are a common find in northern and western Scotland and the Western Isles, and several such finds were made during the nineteenth century at Ballachulish Moss, close to the find spot of the wooden female figure. Groups of families may have gathered together to make these offerings and wooden vessels packed with bog butter would have been valuable gifts.

Across the lowland areas of southern, central and eastern Scotland, impressive items of metalwork were deposited in the wetlands, rivers and caves. Some are personal ornaments, but weapons and horse fittings were also placed in bogs. Sometimes collections of

Wooden Vessel
Wooden vessel from Glen Gill near Morvern, Lochaber. This wooden container was full of bog butter and it is dated to the second or third century AD.
NATIONAL MUSEUMS OF SCOTLAND

What Was Bog Butter?

Bog butter has been found in wooden containers during the digging of peat bogs in a number of places across the north and west Highlands of Scotland and in the Northern and Western Isles. It also occurs in other parts of Europe, for instance in Ireland. It is usually a fairly hard yellow mass when discovered and scientific analysis suggests that it was produced from animal fat. It may have been used for cooking, like modern butter, lard or vegetable oil. It may even have been a cosmetic used as face cream or oil for the hair. It has been suggested that it was placed in the bog in wooden containers in order to improve its taste! Bog butter has been found during modern peat cutting so some at least was deposited and never retrieved. It may have been intended as a gift to the gods to pay them back for providing the community with an agricultural surplus. Although to us it may not appear a very appealing gift, it constituted a valuable commodity in later prehistoric times. The pot with grain from Allt Cleascre on Lewis, discussed on page 23, may be another example of a similar gift.

objects were placed in a bronze cauldron which was lowered into a small loch or boggy hollow. Objects dating from the time between 1500 BC and 700 BC are common and widespread. Later deposits are uncommon until the period of Roman occupation in the late first to third century AD.

Some of the deposits contain massive quantities of valuable metal, as in the case of the ironwork hoards from Carlingwark Loch (Stewartry), Blackburn Mill (Berwickshire) and Eckford (Roxburghshire); it has been suggested that these deposits represent gifts made by large groups of families. Whole communities probably gathered to make these offerings.

Ceremony

Deposition of metal objects in a loch during the ninth or eighth century BC. The objects represent an offering to the gods to ensure success in battle. A range of weapons are shown along with a cauldron into which the weapons will be placed. The cauldron will then be lowered into the loch from the end of the jetty. The man on the jetty is throwing some objects into the loch. A group of onlookers have gathered to observe the ceremony.

DAVID HOGG

Bronze Vessel

A bronze vessel which was put into a peat bog during later prehistory as an offering to the gods. This particularly fine example was found during peat digging at Kincardine Moss, Stirlingshire.

NATIONAL MUSEUMS OF SCOTLAND

the hoards may have been placed in the bog y the head of the community. Alternatively, it is possible that the objects were placed in the bog by a religious leader or druid – perhaps the druid and the head of the community were the same person.

What happened to the dead?

Although it is likely that funerals were iportant times in the cycle of community life, ot know a great deal about how the dead were ne major burial monuments of the Neolithic and Bronze Age – the chambered cairns and substantial burial mounds – were long disused by the late Bronze Age, although new burials were dug into the surface of old mounds until at least 1000 BC. At the beginning of the later prehistoric period there is evidence that bodies were cremated and the ashes buried in simple cairns surrounded by massive kerbs. During the period from 800 BC to AD 200 the dead were not usually placed in formal graves, but sometimes they were dumped into the disused remains of old houses and settlements as at The Howe, described earlier. Occasionally boxes made of stone slabs, or 'cists', were constructed and contain a single body or multiple burials. Evidence from MacArthur's Cave in Argyll, for instance, indicates that dead bodies were also placed in caves.

As well as the occasional burials in cists, caves and disused buildings, pieces of human bone are found within houses, in pits cut into the floors, behind the walls, or under paved surfaces. At The Howe in Orkney, fragments of two human bodies were found in a drain under the floor of the house, while at Cnip in Lewis a small piece of human bone was found in the entrance passage to one of the houses. When a person died the corpse was probably left in the open until the flesh had decayed. Possibly the body was placed on a wooden platform to prevent animals dragging the remains away. In some cultures the period between the death of an individual and the completion of the rotting of their flesh is seen as a journey between life and death, and the consumption of their body by birds is thought to release their spirit; in others the spirit of the dead person is held to be dangerous, particularly to close relatives, until the flesh has rotted. These sorts of beliefs may have been held by our later prehistoric ancestors; there is certainly evidence for exposure of bodies in the Neolithic period, 2000 years or more earlier. The exposure of the body, therefore, may have been considered to be the final stage in the life cycle of the individual, and the parts of the body that

remained were possibly kept by members of the community as symbols of ancestral power.

The direct connection of these remains with the ancestors of the community meant that, on occasions, they were used in interesting ways which reflected their value. At Hornish Point in South Uist, parts of the body of a dead twelve-year-old boy were found divided among four separate pits dug into the floor of a later prehistoric house. It appeared from a study of the remains that this child's body was first exposed and then separated into four quarters to be placed in the pits, along with remains of cattle and sheep. There is no evidence, however, to indicate that the child was sacrificed and he may well have died from natural causes. Possibly the burial of this child was a foundation ritual and the animal bones represented the remains of a meal that accompanied the ritual. Pieces of people were also turned into objects. At Wag of Forse in Caithness three human bones were found: one had been perforated for use as an artefact and a second bone had been used as a peg.

After-death Ceremony

The exposure of a dead man with a woman weeping. The woman's cloak in the picture is based on one which was found in a peatbog in Orkney and is described on p13.
CHRISTINA UNWIN

Human sacrifice

That human sacrifices occurred on occasions has been demonstrated in the case of 'Pete Marsh/Lindow Man', a body found in a peat bog in Cheshire in the 1980s. Such practices also occurred in Scotland. A cave called the Sculptor's Cave at Covesea in Moray, was excavated earlier this century and produced a wide range of later prehistoric artefacts as well as the remains of humans and animals. The human bones indicated that some of the dead had been beheaded, perhaps as an offering to the gods. Human sacrifice was probably an act carried out only when the community was faced with an exceptional crisis such as a seriously failed harvest which threatened its future. Another example may be the sacrifice of captives after victory in battle.

The exposure of dead bodies and the use of pieces of bone from dead relatives shows that later prehistoric communities had very different ways of living from ours; but our practice of secular cremation might appear barbarous to another society – social values and ethics of behaviour vary significantly over space and through time.

The Impact of the People on their Landscape

Through cultivation and the building of their forts and houses our ancestors changed the landscape, and much of their impact is still visible across Scotland, if you know where to look.

The pattern of the landscape

Most of Scotland was occupied during later prehistory. The country would have been a mosaic of different types of land. Cultivation occurred on the fertile coastal soils of the Western Isles, the west and north coast of the mainland and Shetland; inland areas were covered in bogs and forests. Across other parts of the Highlands, river valleys and straths were heavily settled, as were some areas of modern moorland. Other regions were covered by trees or bog. Orkney, Caithness, and the eastern, southern and south-western parts of Scotland were more heavily settled and, in some places, very few trees remained by AD 50. Across the south and east of Scotland large areas had been cleared of trees, while to the north and west forests may have still been extensive. Woodlands, moorland and the coastline edged the settled areas where communities lived and farmed. This cleared land was farmed by families; some was ploughed and some used as pasture.

Bogs and marshes

The heavy rainfall in many parts of western and northern

Land-use Map
The country formed a mosaic of differing land types. This map shows the rough distribution of forest cover around AD 50. In some areas of central Scotland extensive forest cover survived. The northern and western areas had been largely cleared of trees by climatic factors and human activity. The main areas in which people had cleared almost all the trees were to the south and east of the country.

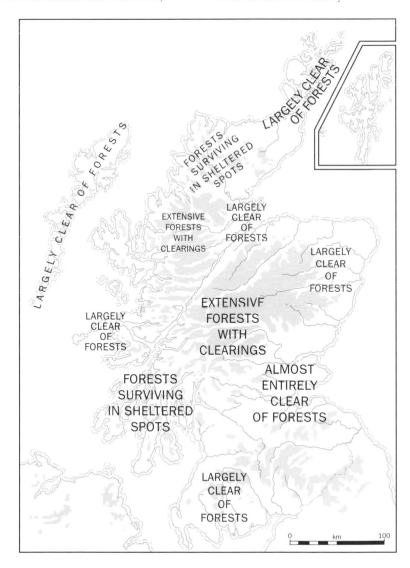

What Other Kinds of Evidence Tell Us About the Past Landscape?

Analysis of pollen found within peat bogs and mires of Scotland has provided us with information about the amount of tree cover and species of trees and plants during the later prehistoric period. Pollen analysis also tells us something of the extent of the peat bogs at this time.

The waterlogged, airless conditions in the bogs preserves vegetable and animal remains due to the fact that the organisms which cause decay cannot live without oxygen. The amount of pollen from different types of plant such as trees and grasses reflects the size of the area covered by woodland or under cultivation. Peat grows in a series of layers which build up through time, the layers of peat below dying and becoming compressed and preserved. These layers can be dated using radiocarbon dating. A peat bog will therefore preserve evidence of the changes in land use around it such as the felling of trees, the regeneration of woodland, the increase in the area of land under agriculture, and even which crops were being grown.

Scotland encouraged the growth of the peat moorland which forms such a distinctive element of the Scottish landscape. Many of these upland peat bogs and some of the lowland bogs, or raised mires, had begun to develop before around 1500 BC. In fact, in some of areas of the west and north we know that bogs started to smother land that had formerly been used for cultivation at this time. These bogs are still fairly common in upland Scotland and were also common in the lowlands before the extensive land drainage campaigns of the eighteenth and nineteenth centuries. For instance, in the central belt of Scotland the area between the modern towns of Aberfoyle and Stirling was covered by a massive bog until it was extensively cleared and drained in the late eighteenth century. During later prehistory the bog would have made travelling across this area very hazardous. Such areas were probably exploited by later prehistoric populations because of their wildlife and because peat could also have been cut for use as fuel.

Forests

It is a modern myth that when the Romans arrived they invaded a largely wooded Scotland occupied by barbaric tribes, but we know from pollen analysis that much of the countryside had already been cleared of trees by that time. The later prehistoric people used the timber to build houses and settlements. Owing to their large-scale clearance across southern Scotland, wood may actually have been hard to obtain; as a result, between 200 BC and AD 200, people had to use more stone to build their houses, settlements and forts. It is likely that people managed the woodland by encouraging the growth of young trees for future structural timbers in certain areas and also by coppicing cut trees, proving that timber formed a valuable resource.

Epilogue – our later prehistoric ancestors

A summary

The evidence for later prehistoric Scotland summarised above demonstrates that people at this time lived in small communities but had widespread contacts with other communities across northern Britain and northern Europe. This is how styles and ideas spread across Scotland.

The main theme in the evidence is the settled agricultural nature of life at this time. The impressive roundhouses and forts of later prehistoric Scotland may suggest that people needed to defend their families, cattle and crops from raiders, but it is also likely that these structures were intended to make an impression – to indicate the power of the individual family who built the house and of the community who worked together to construct the fort. The major hillforts of Scotland may have been places in which large groups of people from a wide area met to exchange goods, tell stories and settle disputes. We have plentiful evidence of houses, settlement, forts and fields, but only limited evidence of how communities disposed of their dead during the Iron Age. We do, however, have some information about their religious beliefs.

The later prehistoric evidence does not suggest that prehistoric Scotland remained the same over the 1700 years covered by this book. In fact, it indicates that families changed their ways through time. At the beginning of our period, the main metal in use was bronze and a range of weapons, tools and ornaments was manufactured from it. By around 700 BC iron had come into use and the creation of iron plough-shares may have enabled families to cultivate heavier, wetter soils. This may have had a dramatic effect on the landscape, as larger areas were cleared for cultivation, demonstrated by the evidence from pollen analysis. In addition, iron weapons were made. These were more effective in killing and maiming humans and animals than bronze weapons and the fact that they may have been used for more aggressive behaviour possibly provides one reason for the building of enclosures around settlements and the construction of large imposing roundhouses.

People also lived in different ways in the different areas of Scotland. For instance, we have seen that a contrast exists between open settlements in Fife and Perthshire and the enclosed settlements of East Lothian and Borders. From 200 BC to AD 200 there was a contrast between the deposition of

Brown Caterthun Hillfort
The hillfort at the Brown Caterthun, Angus. The multiple ramparts of this hillfort are very obvious from the air. This is one of a large number of very well preserved later prehistoric settlements in Scotland which you can visit.
RCAHMS

religious offerings across Scotland – metalwork items were used in the south and east of Scotland and wooden and organic items in the north and west. Numerous differences also occurred in the types of houses and settlements that people built in different parts of Scotland.

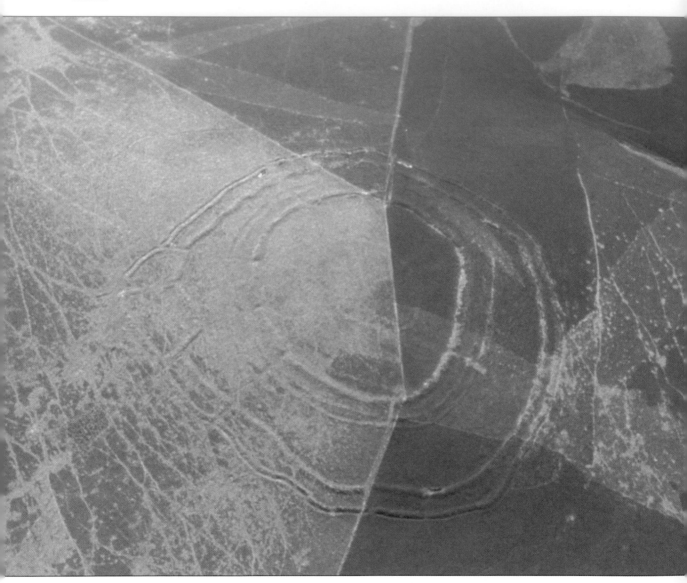

How important is the Scottish evidence?

The evidence for Scotland's later prehistory is particularly important, although there are large gaps in our knowledge about how people lived at this time.

The later prehistoric settlements are particularly significant from a British and European perspective because they are very well preserved. In Highland Scotland, the islands and upland areas of the east, south and south-west there are substantial remains of later prehistoric houses and settlements. When well preserved buildings are excavated they produce particularly important evidence for the domestic life of the people who built and lived in them.

Across much of southern and eastern Britain the majority of sites of later prehistoric date have been flattened by the plough or built over. Modern cultivation methods can destroy much important information, and many sites in southern and eastern Scotland have already been ploughed flat. Ploughing nevertheless does not destroy all of the evidence and the surviving remains of these buildings and sites often demonstrate different ways of life from that of the inhabitants of the north and west of Scotland. We therefore have to preserve and understand later prehistoric sites from the whole of Scotland if we are to maintain a balanced record of our past in the future. The protection of these sites is important because understanding the past illuminates the present and enriches the future.

Lochan Druim an Duin
Lochan Druim an Duin, Sutherland. A substantial roundhouse, possibly a broch, on the north coast of Scotland.
Many later prehistoric settlements are still impressive features of the modern landscape.
DAVID SMITH

How Do I Find Out More?

Sites To Visit

The remains of the later prehistoric people are scattered all over Scotland. Some areas have a range of sites that are excavated and interpreted but most areas have something worth seeing. The list is ordered by area, alphabetically. I have tried to give a broad geographic coverage, concentrating on monuments that are open to the public by Historic Scotland or by other bodies. The initials (HS) means that the site is open to the public by Historic Scotland; (P) means that the monument is opened to the public by another agency. Where there are no initials the site is on private land and the permission of the owner may be required. Ordnance Survey grid references are provided.

Aberdeenshire

Archaeolink – (P) archaeological interpretation centre. This includes the remains of a hillfort, house circle and a modern reconstruction of a roundhouse. Plans exist to build reconstructions of other archaeological monuments in the future.
NJ 667 252.

Angus

Souterrains (all HS)
Ardestie NO 503 344,
Carlungie NO 511 357
and Tealing NO 412 381.

The Brown and White Caterthuns hillforts – (HS) a pair of fine hillforts. Recent excavation has produced later prehistoric dates for the construction of the ramparts.
NO 555 669 and NO 548 661.

Argyll

Kildonan – a small dun or fort which was probably built in later prehistoric times and reoccupied during the Early Historic period.
NR 780 277.

Arran

Torr a'Chaisteal dun – (HS) the remains of a small prehistoric house or fort.
NR 921 232

Berwickshire

Edin's Hall – (HS) – a hillfort, broch and group of hut circles. This is an unusually complex later prehistoric settlement.
NT 773 601

East Lothian

The Chesters – (HS) a heavily fortified hillfort containing traces of later prehistoric houses.
NT 507 782

Traprian Law – (P) a hillfort on the top of a steep-sided hill. Traces of the ramparts of the fort are visible on the north and west faces of the hill and there are faint traces of internal buildings. Excavations produced evidence for Late Bronze Age and Roman period occupation and the finds are in the National Museum of Scotland.
NT 580 747

North Berwick Law – (P) a hillfort located on a steep-sided hill.
NT 556 842

White Castle – a small hillfort.
NT 613 686

Ettrick and Lauderdale

Eildon Hill North – a very extensive hillfort, with traces of ramparts and many internal houses. Evidence for later Bronze Age and Roman-period occupation has been found.
NT 554 328

Inverness

Craig Phadrig – (P) a hillfort which was built and occupied in the later prehistoric period and also under the 'Picts'.
NH 640 453

Kincardineshire

Culsh – (HS) a souterrain.
NJ 504 054

Lewis
Dun Carloway – (HS) a very well preserved broch.
NB 189 412

Lochalsh
Dun Telve broch and Dun Troddan broch – (HS) two very well preserved brochs located close together in Glenelg.
NG 829 172 and NG 833 172.

North Lanarkshire
Castlehill, Barhill – (HS) a small fort close to the line of the Antonine Wall. The ramparts of the fort are difficult to distinguish.
NS 525 726.

Orkney
Gurness – (HS) a very well preserved broch with a surrounding settlement all placed within a encircling rampart.
HY 381 268.

Midhowe – (HS) a very well preserved broch.
HY 371 306.

Souterrains (both HS) Grain (HY 441 116) and Rennibister (HY 397 125).

Perth and Kinross
Kenmore – (P) a reconstructed crannog based on evidence recovered from excavated examples in Loch Tay and elsewhere.
NJ 667 252.

Queen's View – (P) a small homestead which was probably a later prehistoric roundhouse.
NN 863 601.

Ross and Cromarty
Culbokie – (P) a small hillfort.
NH 602 584.

Shetland
Clickhimin – (HS) a broch and settlement on a small island in a loch.
HU 464 408.

Jarlshof – (HS) a broch and settlement. The settlement includes wheelhouses and later Norse and medieval buildings.
HU 398 095.

Mousa – (HS) the best preserved broch, located on a small island.
HU 457 236.

Ness of Burgi – (HS) a small fort of a distinctive type called a 'blockhouse'.
HU 387 083.

Skye
Dun Beag – (HS) the remains of a broch.
NG 339 386.

Sutherland
Carn Liath – (HS) the remains of a broch. Recent excavation has demonstrated that the site was used for hundreds of years before the broch was built.
NC 870 013.

Dun Dornadilla (HS) a broch with an impressive triangular lintel over the entrance.
NC 451 450.

Skelbo Wood – (P) a broch which has not been excavated and survives as an earthwork.
NH 782 944.

West Lothian
Cairnpapple Hill – (HS) this is a Neolithic henge but burials were made into the site during the later prehistoric period.
NS 987 717.

Castlelaw – (HS) an impressive hillfort with a souterrain which was later inserted into the ditch of the fort.
NT 229 638.

Western Isles
Dun Vulan – a broch which has been recently excavated. The excavations indicated areas of settlement outside the wall of the broch.
NF 714 298.

Wigtonshire
Barsalloch – (HS) a small fort or dun.
NX 347 412

Rispain Camp – (HS) a small rectangular fort. Excavation has suggested that it was the home for a later prehistoric community.
NX 429 399.

Further Reading

- The Exploring Scotland's Heritage series published by The Stationary Office explains how to visit various later prehistoric sites in Scotland. Different volumes deal with different areas.

- *Wild Harvesters*, B Finlayson (Canongate 1998), examines the hunter-gatherers of prehistoric Scotland.

- *Farmers, Temples and Tombs*, G Barclay (Canongate 1998), considers the Neolithic and early Bronze Age ancestors of the late prehistoric period.

- *The Ancient Celts*, B Cunliffe (Oxford University Press 1997), is a large, colourful book about Iron Age Europe, which helps to place the Scottish evidence in context.

- *Iron Age Britain*, B Cunliffe (Batsford 1995), is a helpful introductory book with some information about Scotland.

- *Celtic Scotland*, I Armit (Batsford 1997), provides both a fuller study of the evidence than has been possible in this book and a very different approach to the Celts.

- *A Gathering of Eagles*, G Maxwell (Canongate 1998), discusses the Roman invaders.

- *Roman Scotland*, DJ Breeze (Batsford 1996), gives an alternative view about the Roman invaders who came to Scotland.

Acknowledgements

I am very grateful to Fraser Hunter for help with the illustrations and advice on the text; to Ian Armit, Steve Dickinson, Jackie Henrie, Christina Unwin, David Breeze, Niall Sharples and Gordon Barclay for advice on the text and to John Coles, Graeme Wilson and Andrew Fitzpatrick for permission to use various illustrations. Thanks also to Historic Scotland, The Royal Commission on the Ancient Monuments of Scotland and the National Museums of Scotland for permission to use their illustrations. The work of a wide range of authors is quoted in this book, but there has not been space to acknowledge individuals. Much of the evidence quoted is taken from the pages of the *Proceedings of the Society of Antiquaries of Scotland*. Many of the references to the original places of publication can be found in my review article in Volume 122. The maps were prepared by Sylvia Stevenson and Robert Burns.